GIANT POEMS

GIANT POEMS

edited by Daisy Wallace

illustrated by Margot Tomes

HOLIDAY HOUSE • NEW YORK

GRATEFUL ACKNOWLEDGMENT IS MADE TO THE FOLLOWING:

Atheneum Publishers, Inc. for "Bellowed the Ogre" by Lilian Moore from *See My Lovely Poison Ivy*. Text copyright © 1975 by Lilian Moore. Used by permission of Atheneum Publishers.

Basil Blackwell Publisher for "Momotara" translated by Rose Fyleman which appeared in *The Faber Book of Nursery Verse* edited by Barbara Ireson. Copyright 1935 by Rose Fyleman. Reprinted by permission.

Joan Daves for "Giant's Delight" by Steven Kroll. Copyright © 1978 by Holiday House, Inc.

André Deutsch Limited for "Blunderbore" by Roy Fuller from *Poor Roy*. Copyright © 1977. Reprinted by permission.

Harper & Row, Publishers, Inc. for "Me and My Giant" by Shel Silverstein from *Where the Sidewalk Ends*. Copyright © 1974. Reprinted by permission of Harper & Row, Publishers, Inc.

Houghton Mifflin Company for "Like a Giant in a Towel" from *Alligator Pie* by Dennis Lee. Copyright © 1974 by Dennis Lee. Reprinted by permission of Houghton Mifflin Company and The Macmillan Company of Canada Limited.

X.J. Kennedy for "Hickenthrift and Hickenloop." Copyright © 1978 by X.J. Kennedy.

The Literary Trustees of Walter de la Mare and The Society of Authors as their representative for "Grim" by Walter de la Mare. Reprinted by permission.

Little, Brown and Company for "The Greedy Giant" by Laura E. Richards from *Tirra Lirra*. Copyright 1932 by Laura E. Richards. Reprinted by permission.

Macmillan Publishing Co., Inc. for "In the Orchard" from *Collected Poems* by James Stephens. Copyright 1915 by Macmillan Publishing Co., Inc., renewed 1943 by James Stephens. Reprinted by permission of Macmillan Publishing Co., Inc. and The Macmillan Publishing Company of Canada Limited.

McIntosh and Otis, Inc. for "A Giant Named Stanley" by Michael Patrick Hearn. Copyright © 1978 by Michael Patrick Hearn.

Jack Prelutsky for "Huffer and Cuffer." Copyright © 1978 by Jack Prelutsky.

Rita Scott for "Magic Story For Falling Asleep" by Nancy Willard. Copyright © 1978 by Nancy Willard.

Dorothy Brown Thompson for "Shrieks at Midnight," published first in *St. Nicholas Magazine,* and copyright reassigned to Dorothy Brown Thompson. Used by permission of Dorothy Brown Thompson.

Library of Congress Cataloging in Publication Data

Main entry under title:

Giant poems.

SUMMARY: Sixteen poems about giants by a variety of authors.

1. Giants—Juvenile poetry. [1. Giants—Poetry.
2. American poetry—Collections. 3. English poetry—Collections] I. Wallace, Daisy. II. Tomes, Margot.
PZ8.3.G34   811´.008´0375   77-21038
ISBN 0-8234-0326-2

For Alexander Valenti

CONTENTS

FE, FI, FO, FUM

Fe, fi, fo, fum,
I smell the blood of an Englishman!
Be he alive or be he dead,
I'll grind his bones to make my bread!

ANONYMOUS

GRIM

Beside the blaze of forty fires
    Giant Grim doth sit,
Roasting a thick-wooled mountain sheep
    Upon an iron spit.
Above him wheels the winter sky,
    Beneath him, fathoms deep,
Lies hidden in the valley mists
    A village fast asleep—
Save for one restive hungry dog
    That, snuffing towards the height,
Smells Grim's broiled supper-meat, and spies
    His watch-fire twinkling bright.

WALTER DE LA MARE

9

IN THE ORCHARD

There was a giant by the Orchard Wall
Peeping about on this side and on that,
And feeling in the trees. He was as tall
As the big apple tree, and twice as fat:
His beard poked out, all bristly-black, and there
Were leaves and gorse and heather in his hair.

He held a blackthorn club in his right hand,
And plunged the other into every tree,
Searching for something—You could stand
Beside him and not reach up to his knee,
So big he was—I trembled lest he should
Come trampling, round-eyed, down to where I stood.

I tried to get away—But, as I slid
Under a bush, he saw me, and he bent
Down deep at me, and said, *"Where is she hid?"*
I pointed over there, and off he went—

But, while he searched, I turned and simply flew
Round by the lilac bushes back to you.

JAMES STEPHENS

BLUNDERBORE

The giant Blunderbore,
About to dine on pork,
Called in a blunderborian roar:
"Bring me my knife and fork!"

And in four servants ran,
Trotting for dear life:
At each end of the fork one man,
And two men to the knife.

"Goodness," one captive cried,
"This giant's awfully big.
But I'd be still more terrified
To meet a giant's pig."

ROY FULLER

A GIANT NAMED STANLEY

I ain't one to complain,
Don't get me wrong;
Something's been buggin' me
For far too long.
My mother's an angel,
My father—a saint!
And in all of these years,
I've but one complaint.
I love my mother,
My father I prize;
But why did they give
A kid of my size
    The gentle name of Stanley?
In the fabled days of yore,
Our tribe was famed for blood and gore:
    Cormoran and Blunderbore,
    Blunderbeard and Thunderoar,
    Gog, Magog, Asundertore!
    But not a single Stanley.
I'd have taken Blunderbore,
Shuttlecock or Battledore,
Close-your-mouth or Shut-the-door!
    Anything but Stanley!
    Oh, anything but Stanley!

MICHAEL PATRICK HEARN

13

SHRIEKS AT MIDNIGHT

I do like ogres—
There's something about them
So utterly ruthless
And yet absurd!
    I don't believe in them,
Yet I shiver
The very instant
I hear the word—
FE–FI–FO–FUM!

DOROTHY BROWN THOMPSON

14

BELLOWED THE OGRE

Bellowed the Ogre
With One Fiery Eye,
    "Ho!
    The Mightiest
    Monster
    Am
    I!"

Roared Dinosaur Rex,
"I'm not easy to vex,
    But I'll swat
    That
    Braggart
    When he goes
    By!"

Whispered the Wizard,
"Upon my gizzard!
    I'll make
    Ogre a
    Bullfrog
    And
    Rex a
    Lizard!"

LILIAN MOORE

ME AND MY GIANT

I have a friend who is a giant,
And he lives where the tall weeds grow.
He's high as a mountain and wide as a barn,
And I only come up to his toe, you know,
    I only come up to his toe.

When the daylight grows dim I talk with him
Way down in the marshy sands,
And his ear is too far away to hear,
But still he understands, he 'stands,
    I know he understands.

For we have a code called the "scratch-tap code,"
And here is what we do—
I scratch his toe . . . once means, "Hello"
And twice means, "How are you?"
Three means, "Does it look like rain?"
Four times means, "Don't cry."
Five times means, "I'll scratch you a joke."
And six times means, "Goodbye," "Goodbye,"
    Six times means, "Goodbye."

And he answers me by tapping his toe—
Once means, "Hello, friend."
Two taps means, "It's very nice
    to feel your scratch again."

17

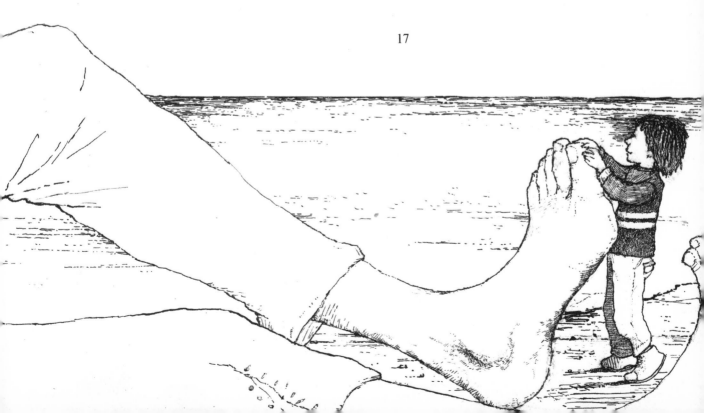

Three taps means, "It's lonely here
     with my head in the top of the sky."
Four taps means, "Today an eagle
     smiled as she flew by."
Five taps means, "Oops, I just bumped
     my head against the moon."
Six means, "Sigh" and seven means, "Bye"
And eight means, "Come back soon, soon, soon."
     Eight means, "Come back soon."

And then I scratch a thousand times,
And he taps with a bappity-bimm,
And he laughs so hard he shakes the sky—
     That means I'm tickling him!

SHEL SILVERSTEIN

18

GIANT'S WIFE

The terrible giant had a wife
    Who was almost twelve feet tall.
She slept with her head in the kitchen
    And her feet way out in the hall.

ANONYMOUS

19

GIANTS' DELIGHT

Vats of soup
On table trays
Side of shark
With mayonnaise
Haunch of ox
With piles of mice
Mounds of gristle
Served on ice
Bone of mammoth
Head of boar
Whales and serpents
By the score
Tons of cole slaw
Stacks of rabbits
(Giants have such
Piggy habits)
Then, at last,
There comes a stew
Full of buffalo
And ewe
Followed by
Some chocolate cakes
Big enough
For stomachaches

STEVEN KROLL

THE GREEDY GIANT

There once was a giant
So far from compliant,
    He wouldn't eat toast with his tea.
"A substance so horrid
Brings pains in my forehead,
    And aches in my toe-toes," said he, said he,
    "And aches in my toe-toes," said he.

They brought him a tartlet
To cheer up his heartlet,
    They brought him both jelly and jam;
But still while he gobbled,
He signed and he sobbled,
    "You *don't* know how hungry I am, I am,
    You don't *know* how hungry I am!"

They brought him a cruller
To make him feel fuller,
    They brought him some pancakes beside,
They brought him a muffin,
On which he was stuffin',
    When all of a sudden he died, he died,
    When all of a sudden he died.

LAURA E. RICHARDS

21

GIANT CHANTS

"Whoever shall this trumpet blow,
Shall soon the giant overthrow,
And break the black enchantment straight;
So all shall be in happy state."

from *Jack the Giant-Killer*

22

Do what you can to get away,
Or you'll become the Giant's prey;
He's gone to fetch his brother, who
Will likewise kill and torture you!

Tho' here you lodge with me this night,
You shall not see the morning light,
My club will dash your brains out quite.

from *The History of Jack & The Giants*
(early 1700s)

HICKENTHRIFT AND HICKENLOOP

Hickenthrift and Hickenloop
    Stood fourteen mountains high:
They'd wade the wind, they'd have to stoop
    To let the full moon by.

Their favorite sport, played on a court,
    Was called Kick Down the Castle:
They'd stamp their boots, those vast galoots,
    Till king lay low as vassal.

One day while spooning hot rock soup
    From a volcano crater,
Said Hickenthrift, "Hey, Hickenloop,
    Who of us two is greater?"

Across the other's jagged brow
    Dark thunder seemed to drift,
And Hickenloop, with one swift swoop,
    Ate straight through Hickenthrift.

                    X.J. KENNEDY

MOMOTARA

Where did Momotara go,
With a hoity-toity-tighty?
He went to lay the giants low,
The wicked ones and mighty.

What did Momotara take?
His monkey, dog and pheasant,
Some dumplings and an almond cake,
Which made the journey pleasant.

26

How did Momotara fare
Upon the fearful meeting?
He seized the giants by the hair
And gave them all a beating.

What did Momotara bring?
Oh, more than you could measure:
A silver coat, a golden ring
And a wagon-load of treasure.

What did Momotara do?
He sat himself astride it;
The monkey pushed, the pheasant drew
And the little dog ran beside it.

A Japanese nursery rhyme
translated by ROSE FYLEMAN

HUFFER AND CUFFER

Huffer, a giant ungainly and gruff
encountered a giant called Cuffer.
said Cuffer to Huffer, I'M ROUGH AND I'M TOUGH,
said Huffer to Cuffer, I'M TOUGHER.

they shouted such insults as BOOB and BUFFOON
and OVERBLOWN BLOWHARD and BLIMP
and BLUSTERING BLUBBER and BLOATED BALLOON
and SHATTERBRAIN, SHORTY and SHRIMP.

28

then Huffer and Cuffer exchanged mighty blows,
they basted and battered and belted,
they chopped to the neck and they bopped in the nose
and they pounded and pummeled and pelted.

they pinched and they punched and they smacked
        and they whacked
and they rocked and they socked and they smashed,
and they rapped and they slapped and they
        throttled and thwacked
and they thumped and they bumped and they bashed.

they cudgeled each other on top of the head
with swipes of the awfulest sort,
and now they are no longer giants, instead
they both are exceedingly short.

                                    JACK PRELUTSKY

LIKE A GIANT IN A TOWEL

When the wind is blowing hard
Like a giant in the yard,
    I'm glad my bed is warm;
    I'm glad my bed is warm.

When the rain begins to rain
Like a giant with a pain,
    I'm glad my bed is warm;
    I'm glad my bed is warm.

When the snowstorm starts to howl
Like a giant in a towel,
    I'm glad my bed is warm;
    I'm glad my bed is warm.

30

And when the giants realize
That no one's scared of their disguise,
They go to bed and close their eyes—
    They're glad their beds are warm;
    They're glad their beds are warm.

DENNIS LEE

MAGIC STORY
FOR FALLING ASLEEP

When the last giant came out of his cave
and his bones turned into the mountain
and his clothes turned into the flowers,

nothing was left but his tooth
which my dad took home in his truck
which my granddad carved into a bed

which my mom tucks me into at night
when I dream of the last giant
when I fall asleep on the mountain.

NANCY WILLARD